THE FANTASY OF PIETER BRUEGHEL

THE
FANTASY
OF
PIETER

BRVEGHEL

ADRIAAN J. BARNOUW

LEAR PUBLISHERS NEW YORK

COPYRIGHT 1947 BY LEAR PUBLISHERS INC.
24 EAST 11TH STREET   NEW YORK 3, N. Y.
MANUFACTURED IN THE UNITED STATES OF AMERICA

THE FANTASY OF PIETER BRUEGHEL

PIETER BRUEGHEL was a lonely pioneer in the age of the Reformation, and his art a reaction against the style and the aesthetic standards of his time. The Italian manner was then in vogue in the Netherlands, large canvases full of contorted figures, dull in coloring, false in pathos. The artists who catered to this taste were kept busy by the demand for such pictures from Spain. Brueghel, as many others of his Dutch fellow craftsmen, made the Italian journey in the early fifties, but he came back unconverted to the Italian style. His art was a reaction of native realism against foreign influence, an aesthetic revolt coinciding with the people's revolt against Spanish rule. He drove the nude heroes and gods of classical mythology off the canvas and painted in their stead the native crowd with naked realism. Humanistic culture, with its hero worship, its cult of Latin, and its contempt for the vulgar, found a formidable antagonist in Brueghel, who with his brush spoke a language that was pure plastic Dutch.

Brueghel's art was not only an aesthetic but also a social protest. "You cannot help laughing at the droll figures that he painted," says Carel van Mander, his earliest biographer. But I, for one, find it difficult to laugh at his drolleries. Disfigured shapes, hunchbacks, cripples, blind beggars, drunkards, idiots, epileptics, legless grotesques, all the human wreckage of a time that was out of joint were rendered by him with poignant realism. The pain and the pity that stirred within him at the spectacle of their ugliness found expression in the beauty of their portrayal.

His own features had nothing in common with the types that he preferred to paint. A finely cut profile, a high forehead, and a dreamy expression are the striking traits of that noble face. By the testimony of that portrait, a contemporary copper plate, Pieter Brueghel, though of peasant stock, was akin to the great visionaries and thinkers of the Reformation period, himself a reformer of social and artistic consciousness.

Brueghel was a native of the Duchy of Brabant and lived in the middle of the sixteenth century, from about 1530 to 1569. Little is known of his life. A generation after his death Carel van Mander, the author of "The Lives of the Dutch Painters," published the story that had come to him by word of mouth. He was usually well informed and did his best to collect reliable data. But an account that travels through time by oral transmission is apt, during a thirty-years' voyage, to collect accretions, like barnacles that cling to the keel of a ship. It is impossible now to scrape off the barnacles, unless official records of the period should flatly disprove the accuracy of Van Mander's statements. But that is not the case. Only a few details of his biography are subject to doubt because they are not confirmed by the records.

He was mistaken in saying that Brueghel was born in a village of that name not far from Breda. There is a village of Brueghel near the town of Eindhoven, south of 's-Hertogenbosch; there is none near Breda. Guicciardini, an Italian resident of Antwerp, who published during Brueghel's lifetime an accurate "Description of the Low Countries," called the artist "Pietro Brueghel di Breda." The Brueghel family, doubtless, originated in the village that gave them their name, but they had evidently left it before the birth of Pieter. Since both Guicciardini and Van Mander mention Breda in connection with his birth, he probably saw the light of day in that ancient city.

He was registered, says Van Mander, as a member of the artists' guild at Antwerp in 1551, and the records bear him out. If he started his apprenticeship, as was customary, at the age of twelve, and took from six to eight years to master his craft, he must have been born around 1530. Van Mander states that he was a pupil of Pieter Koeck van Aelst. There is no record that confirms this, and the lack of even the slightest affinity between the styles of Koeck and Brueghel casts additional doubt on this tradition. Brueghel married a daughter of Koeck's, and it may be that Van Mander took it for granted that the relationship between father and son-in-law had developed, as so often happened in those days, from that between master and pupil.

It is more likely that the young Brueghel received his early training in a workshop where the manner of Hieronymus Bosch was an honored tradition. Bosch himself cannot have been his master; he died in 1516, before Brueghel was born. But his fame was still fresh and young. Pieter, who was like Bosch a Brabanter born, must have revered the memory of his celebrated countryman. Bosch had lived and worked in the Brabant city that is officially known by the cumbrous name of 's-Hertogenbosch. But no Dutchman ever calls it that. Den Bosch is its name in popular parlance, and Hieronymus, the painter, received his second name from the city that he had honored with his art. What more natural than that Pieter's parents should have apprenticed the boy to a master who had been close to Hieronymus and carried on his tradition at Den Bosch?

The engravings reproduced in this volume are convincing proof that Brueghel's art was grafted on that of Hieronymus Bosch. One of them, "The Big Fishes Eat the Little Ones," bears the statement "Hieronijmus Bos. inventor." The engraver used as his model a drawing that Brueghel copied after Bosch. That copy is still extant and bears the signature "Bruegel 1556." The engraver required a special line technique in the drawing that he followed and that was what young Brueghel supplied to the production of this print. He acted as intermediary between Bosch and the engraver.

The publisher of most of these engravings was Hieronymus Cock, an artist who had abandoned the painter's craft to become an art dealer and publisher of prints. Cock's father had been a close friend of Bosch, and since he bears the latter's Christian name it is not unlikely that Hieronymus Cock was the old master's godchild. He seems to have had drawings by Bosch, including the Fishes, in his possession, which, thanks to that relationship, he may have obtained from the master's studio after the latter's death.

The Fishes print is a rare instance of Brueghel supplying a copy after Bosch to the engraver. He was capable of original work for the engraver's guidance. The earliest composition from his hand in this collection is "The Temptation of St. Anthony," which was published by Cock in 1556. It is a clumsy copy, the work, evidently, of an unskilled craftsman, far inferior to the Fishes print, which appeared the year after. The latter engraving was the work of Pieter van der Heyden. In him Cock had found the right man for the difficult job, and from the moment that he entered Cock's employ, in 1559, the imposing series of prints after Brueghel's original designs began to appear. Not all of them, though, were engraved by Van der Heyden. Cock himself was no mean craftsman and may have transferred some of Brueghel's drawings to the copper plate. Others who made them available in printed copies were Pieter Huys, Philippe Galle, and Jan Wierix. The subjects were probably assigned to the artist by the publisher. But

Brueghel was evidently given perfect freedom to express in their execution his own philosophy of life.

The world to him was a scene of folly. That was a popular theme both in literature and art since Erasmus published his "Praise of Folly."

Brueghel did not preach, but looked at the folly of his fellow men as a phenomenon that was a natural and intrinsic part of life. In the series of the Cardinal Sins he adopted, it is true, the teaching of the medieval Church, which assigned to each sin its retribution in hell. But his delight in picturing diabolical creatures need not reflect an orthodox belief in their reality. On the contrary, his scepticism made it possible for him to give free vent to his imagination.

It does not follow, however, that Brueghel had left the Church of Rome. We moderns are apt to make the mistake of transferring the sharp cleavages between present-day denominations to the period in which these took their rise. The age of the Reformation did not see them distinctly circumscribed. There were preachers and theorists who expounded their heterodoxies, but the people to whom they addressed them were not clear in their minds as to where they stood. Brueghel is believed to have joined the Family of Love, a harmless sect that was founded by Hendrik Nicolas, who taught that all religions are symbols of one truth and that Holy Writ had only an allegorical meaning. The members, known by the name of Familists, or Nicolaites, had no meeting places; the bond between them was maintained by occasional visits of Nicolas, who combined his business journeys with his apostolic labors. He had followers among the humanists at Antwerp, and Brueghel too may have felt attracted toward the humane teachings of this itinerant evangelist. But there is no definite proof that he ever was a member of his devout Family.

It is clear from these engravings that Brueghel knew the scriptures intimately. I believe that many a cryptic detail of his crowded compositions can be explained with the help of a bible text. The allusion is often made in a casual, offhand manner as if he were sure that it would be recognized without fail by an audience steeped in biblical lore. In "The Temptation of St. Anthony" an archer up in the tree above the hermitage is aiming his arrow at the saint. King David is seen playing the harp in the depth of the hollow trunk; search then in the Psalms for the man with the crossbow. And indeed, in the eleventh psalm you will find, "Lo, the wicked bend their bow, they make ready their arrow upon the string, that they may privily shoot at the upright in heart."

Current local events, unprinted stage plays of the Rhetoricians, popular jokes and song hits of the day may also have left visible reflections in subordinate incidents of Brueghel's drawings; the ephemeral nature of such allusions baffles all attempts at interpretation. Even the proverbs, which the artist loved to turn into pictures, cannot always be identified, for not all of them have been recorded in print and few have remained in current usage.

The notes to these prints, therefore, do not constitute an exhaustive commentary. But they will enable the reader to look at them with a clearer understanding of their import and thus enhance his enjoyment of Brueghel's art. It is an art that mirrors the life of the simple folk he loved with a vividness such as few other artists have achieved. If he had produced nothing else than the original drawings for these engravings, he could, on the strength of this graphic output, lay claim to being ranked among the greatest masters of the Dutch school.

Adriaan J. Barnouw

THE ENGRAVINGS

ANGER MAKES THE MOUTH swell, embitters the mind, troubles the spirit, blackens the blood." The crowded scene is a medley of all the mental aberrations and obscene cruelties of which angry man is capable. He is depicted in the swollen-mouthed warrior in the left foreground who brandishes a spiked club, which the Dutch ironically called a *goedendag,* a good-day. Under the penthouse behind him a human monster with a hog-like snout is roasting his victim over a woodfire and pouring molten lead upon his body. On the top of the army tent to the right a man and a woman are being boiled in an iron cauldron over a coal fire, and out of this apparently fire-proof tent a troop of mad soldiers emerge who with a gigantic knife cut the naked bodies of sprawling men and women in two. The Virago in armor who eggs them on with sword and flaming torch is Anger herself. Inside the barrel, in the centre, a cutthroat is doing his blood deed. A murderous hag with a knife between her teeth, her right arm in a sling, and a bottle of poison in her left hand, dominates this scene of anger with her gigantic figure. Anger incites to wars and turns the warriors into devils who walk on stumps and vultures' claws and drag a dragon's tail behind. Angry men are no better than beasts of prey, than the wolf, the bear, the hawk. The wages of anger are the fire and the gallows. The ship of fools hoisted on top of a pair of barrels is an emblem of this anger-maddened world. And all these crazed fools, if they could only control their anger, might share the happy lot of the two fishermen in the far background who, by the side of the town on fire, present a picture of perfect tranquillity.

.P. brueghel. Inuentor.   IRA   .H. Cock. excudeb. Cum gratia et pniuilegio . 1 5 5 8 .

ORA   TVMENT   IRA,,   NIGRESCVNT   SANGVINE   VENÆ

Gramscap doet den mont swillen / en verbittert den moet Sij beroert den gheest / en maeckt swert dat bloet

SLOTH MAKES A MAN weak and dries up his sinews until he is no longer fit for anything." Thus says the Flemish text that goes with the picture. The thought is better expressed by the saying, "Sloth like rust consumes faster than labor wears." The print repeats the lesson over and over again by showing in a variety of scenes the corrosive effect of sloth in illustrations of proverbial wisdom, some of which elude all attempts at interpretation. The centre is occupied by Sloth herself, a sleeping woman reclining against the body of a sleeping donkey, the animal which, most unjustly, is considered to be an embodiment of sloth. *Asino pigrior,* lazier than a donkey, was a common saying in ancient Rome. The snail is another one, and snails of various sizes are seen crawling across the picture, a giant one leading a lazy rider a snail's pace in the background. The indecent figure in the centre alludes to the vulgar description of a man who is the superlative of laziness: "He is too lazy to shit." A Dutch proverb calls laziness the devil's pillow, and a devil is shown presenting a pillow to the woman who, instead of putting a meal on the table for her two lazy jackanapes of sons, is dozing with her head upon her hand. A demon with a wolfish snout is doing a similar service to dame Sloth. The same thought is expressed by the proverb "A pillow does not lead to heaven," and the loafer who, like a pap-eating baby, is pulled in a perambulator by a stork in monk' clothes will certainly not reach St. Peter's gate. The rat b his side must be a dormouse, who is also a proverbial lazy bones. In Dutch he is called *slaapmuis* (sleep-mouse) an the first part of his English name is probably the stem o the Latin verb *dormire* (to sleep). The slothful, who hav time on their hands, are easily tempted to dicing and whor ing. A grinning demon invites the lazy woman at th empty dining table to come to the bed behind the curtain There, under cover of the night, the hoot-owl's hour, sh can escape her boredom in his fanglike arms. Above thi scene hangs a clockwork and a man on top of it seems en tangled in its mechanism. Man *is* a clockwork and need winding up, otherwise sloth will bring him to a stop. H is striking a bell similar in shape to the ones that are sus pended from the branch above his head. *Luien* is the wor in Dutch for tolling the bell, and *luien* means also "Laz people." The hatchet that, like a signboard, hangs out o the crazy roof is the one that, according to the proverb, th lazy carpenter is looking for. And why does the hand o the dial in the left background point at eleven? Elever says the proverb, is the fool's number; lazy fools are ap to postpone the work they must do till the eleventh hou But delay, like a rising tide, swallows up time and leave the slothful defenceless and naked in their need.

DESIDIA

brueghel Inuentor

H·Cock excud cum priuleg 1558

SEGNITIES ROBVR FRANGIT, LONGA OCIA NERVOS.

Traegheyt maeckt machteloos en verdroocht Die senuwen dat de mensch niewers toe en doocht

PRIDE OCCUPIES the centre foreground. She is a magnificently dressed old harridan who is admiring herself in a handmirror. But the reflexion in the glass shows a monkey's face. She is accompanied by her traditional attribute, the peacock proudly displaying his splendid plumage.

The proverb says, "Where pride and luxury lead the way, shame and poverty bring up the rear"; so Pride is followed by a naked woman in the midst of a group of people whose shame can be read in their faces: a few are human, but the others are beaks of birds or snouts of swine. The surrounding architecture in this proud men's hell is a nightmarish satire on the conspicuous waste indulged in by the proud upon this earth; the roofs are ludicrous contraptions apparently suggested by contemporary fashions in headgear. Conspicuous among these buildings is a gigantic breastplate surmounted by a helmet with open vizard, in which a swarm of naked souls are appearing as supplicants before a helmeted man, who seems to be acting as their judge. In the foreground an acrobatic devil with an arrow in his back performs an act that parodies Dame Pride's self-admiration: he is looking at the reflection of his arse in an octagonal mirror. The Dutch say of a braggard: *Hy zet een grooten bek op* (he opens a big mouth). That is what the two men to the left are doing. They are making so much noise that a third person in the group has to hold his ears.

The punishment that is awaiting them is a padlock on their lips such as locks the mouth of the monster in the foreground, a man's head rising out of a breastplate which turns into a fish's body with a peacock's feather for a tail. This silenced head looks at itself in a mirror held up to him by a mermaid in a nun's habit. She points with her right hand at the braggards behind her as if saying to the padlocked head, "This is the punishment that awaits those two." To the right is a sixteenth-century barbershop and beauty parlor. In front of it an assistant with a wolf's snout is giving a woman a shampoo, indoors the boss administers a facial treatment to a customer. Above the entrance hangs the diploma certifying that the barber is licensed to practise surgery; the pestle and mortar proclaim him to be an apothecary as well. The lute on the outside wall was an essential part, in Brueghel's days, of a barbershop's equipment: the clients who had to wait their turn could while away the time by practising on the instrument. The man on the roof who is defiling this place of body culture translates into action the common people's verbal contempt for such vanity: *daar scheit ik op* (I shit on that) they will say. In the far background is shown an illustration of the proverb, "Pride comes before a fall." A Dutch rhyme says, *Hovaardij, wat plaagt gij mij!* (Pride, how you plague me!) The legend underneath the picture sums it all up this way, "The proud do not love the gods, nor the gods the proud."

SVPERBIA

.P. breughel. Inuentor.

NEMO   SVPERBVS   AMAT   SVPEROS,   NEC   AMATVR   AB   ILLIS.
Houerdije   werdt   van   godt   bouen   al   ghehaet   Tseghelije   werdt   godt   weder   van   houerdije   versmaet

S CRAPING AVARICE has no regard for honor, courtesy, shame, or divine warning." That is the meaning of the Dutch words under the picture. The Latin is more succinct: "Has the grasping miser ever any fear or shame?" Avarice is seated in the centre, a haughty lady who has her eyes fixed on the gold in her lap and her right hand groping in the money chest which a demon is filling with coins out of a broken jar. She wears the fifteenth-century headdress whose horns, according to contemporary moralists, were the hide-out of devils. The toad at her feet is her counterpart among the beasts for, says Cesare Ripa in his "Iconologia," the toad feeds on sand and dust, of which there is plenty, yet abstains from it lest there shoul[d] not be enough. The usurer has no compassion. The nake[d] bring him their last possessions though the sign he hang[s] out is a pair of scissors that catches his victims between th[e] blades. The architecture, as in all Brueghel's pictures [of] the cardinal sins, anticipates the fantastic absurdities [of] Hollywood. This world of greedy fools is a scene of blatan[t] insanity. The miser is the captive of his own greed, as in[-] capable of enjoyment as the shark in the glass cage on th[e] usurer's roof. For his wealth is always the target of th[e] envious. It is stolen by burglars, seized by a plunderin[g] mob, consumed by fire. The miser's lot, indeed, is misery[.]

AVARITIA

R brueghel Inuentor   Cock excud cum priuileg 1558

QVIS   METVS ,   AVT   PVDOR   EST   VNQVAM   PROPERANTIS   AVARI?
Ewe beleestheyt scaemte noch gallyck vermaen En siet die scrapende ghierichheyt niet aen

GLUTTONY is personified by a bibulous fat monk. He is seated on top of a hog whose ears and hoofs are those of an ass. Another hoglike demon brings him a fresh supply of liquor. All around are scenes of infernal horror. If the visual realization of the punishments awaiting hoglike gluttons in hell can act as a deterrent, Brueghel's picture must have had a wholesome effect in his day. "Avoid drunkenness and over-eating," says the accompanying text, "for excess causes man to forget God and himself." The glutton forgets himself to the extent of turning into the food or drink that he covets: the voracious fish-eater into a fish, like the man in the right foreground whose swollen belly has split the skin and had to be stitched, or like the drunkard behind him who has turned into a barrel. Another is forced to cart his bloated abdomen around on a wheelbarrow. But hell varies its tortures to fit the many varieties of the cardinal sin: the drunkard who could not learn to hold his liquor is condemned to eternal vomiting; two other filthy soaks have to bathe in the foul matter that he belches forth. One of these two is atoning for the unsteadiness of his gait while alive by balancing an egg on his head.

The flour mill and the oven that had to feed the gluttons on earth are turned into the instruments of their torture: they must in turn feed the mill with their bodies, they are used as fuel for the infernal oven. And worst punishment, perhaps, of all: the Tantalus torture of the glutton who, firmly immured inside a block of stone and riveted to its walls with an axle drilled through his head from ear to ear, must watch the hellish drinking bout in front of him. The bagpipe, emblem of bloated gluttony, is hanging deflated in the barren tree.

GVLA.

R.
AC.

H. Cock excud cum gratia et privilegio. 1558

EBRIETAS EST VITANDA, INGLVVIESQVE . CIBORVM

Schout dronckenschap en gulsichsyck eten Want ouerdaet doet godt en hem seluen vergheten.

ENVY ACCOMPANIED by her attribute, the turkey, is seated on a stone bench in front of a hollow tree whose antler-shaped branches grow into turkey feathers. Behind her stands a demon who holds a mock coronet above her head. The morsel that she is bringing to her mouth is probably her own heart, for—says the Dutch legend—Envy is a beast that eats itself. To the left of her a she-devil, with a stag's head, the garb of cuckoldry, is tempting a woman with an apple, the apple of discord.

The most striking feature of this print is the display of footwear. The foot is a measure of man's moral conduct. The Dutch say of the rich who make a display of their wealth that "they live on a large foot" (*Zij leven op grooten voet*). Social inequality is measured in terms of footwear by the proverb, *De man in laarzen kent den man in schoen-en niet* (the man in boots does not know the man in shoes).

The shoemaker shop occupies part of a circular space which is surrounded by a stone wall. In the centre of this enclosure stands a cracked globe partly embedded in the ground. It is surmounted by a helmet-like ornament which carries, as in armorial bearings, a pair of swaying legs for a crest. One leg is booted and spurred, the other is merely dressed in hose. The booted leg hurls itself upward, the other is caught in a sling and is being pulled down by the crowd below. There is as little co-ordination between the booted and the bootless leg as there is companionship between the man in boots and the man in shoes of the proverb.

The corollary of pride ignoring poverty is the poor man's envy of the rich. Envy's arrow is seen piercing the booted leg. In front of the shoemaker's booth a line of naked souls is waiting to be fitted for the walk of life. But a hellish satellite of Envy is hatching mischief and arousing envy of the large-footed man in the others. The shoemaker, one of the itinerant class, carries his ware in a huge basket, which is standing under the shelf in the booth. A less successful fellow craftsman has been reduced to keeping shop in his shoe hamper. He has hung out a shoe as a signboard and is waiting in vain for customers. The shoe on his head is a token of his failure. *Hij is met de kous op den kop thuisgekomen* (he has come home with the hose on his head) is a proverbial picture, still in common use, of a man frustrated in his enterprise. Envious of his competitor he covers his left eye so as not to see the other's custom-crowded booth; with the other he watches the monster that is eating one of his shoes, an infernal embodiment of his sin. In the city moat a barge is floating with a corpse on board that has its head encased, as in a tight collar, within a miniature replica of the boat. The dead man's abdomen is a gaping hole from which branches are sprouting that attract the birds. The meaning of this surrealistic fantasy is explained by the Dutch legend underneath the picture. "Envy," it says, "is an immortal death and cruel plague, a beast that eats itself with vicious torment." Envy's dead body is immortal, witness the new life that branches from the corpse.

INVIDIA

INVIDIA HORRENDVM MONSTRVM, SÆVISSIMA PESTIS
Een onsterffelijcke doot es nijt en wreede peste Een beest die haer seluen eet met valschen moleste

LUST PERSONIFIED by a naked woman is being fondled and kissed by a demon with a hoglike snout. They are seated inside a huge hollow tree, one of whose boughs has the shape of an antlered stag. Lust is exemplified in several other animals: the dog, the frog, the monkey, the rooster. The apples that grow on the antler's branches are emblems of lust because of their resemblance to woman's breasts. From the dark recess of the hollow tree a demon emerges to offer an aphrodisiac to the revolting couple. In the centre foreground a bodyless head whose mouth is at the same time its arse holds with its leg-arms a knifed egg over itself and lets its contents drip on its face. The procession that passes by at the back of the tree is a hellish parody of the popular punishment meted out to an adulterer by his fellow townsmen. They paraded him through the streets on a horse or ass with a paper pinned to his hat proclaiming the sin for which he suffered. Bagpipe music heads the procession in hell as upon earth, but the culprit's mount in hell is a skeleton and infernal monsters do the beating. The two nude women in their midst, the adulterer's accomplices no doubt, must follow in the track of his shame. In the background the artist has depicted earthly allurements to lust, such as a love bower, a fountain of youth, and a mill that grinds old women into young maidens. The two horned women on the lawn are procuresses who pander to men's lust. The bower of love seems a place of enchantment, but the delights that it offers are as futile and transitory as the colors of a soap bubble. That seems to be the moral of the scene in the mussel shell on top of the hollow tree. "Lust stinks," says the Dutch text to the picture, "and is full of impurity; she breaks man's strength and weakens the limbs." She breaks them as relentlessly as the giant pike that has suddenly leapt out of the moat crushes his victims on the bridge between his jaws.

LUST.

LVXVRIA   ENERVAT   VIRES,   EFFOEMINAT   ARTVS.

Luxurÿe stinckt sÿ is vol onsuuerheden Sÿ breeckt die Crachten en sÿ swackt die leden

PATIENCE, LIKE St. Anthony in his hermitage, remains unmoved by the nightmarish visions that surround her. She rests upon the solid base of Hope that is anchored to the ground and puts her trust in the cross of Christ. It is doubtful whether each detail carries a special meaning. Brueghel delighted in giving free vent to his fertile imagination while in the act of designing compositions such as this. He loved to invent amphibious creatures, men who are monkeys, fishes that are boats, birds that are dragons, eggs that are men. The hollow tree is a stock requisite in his phantastic stage settings. This one harbors a nest of iniquities. Wine is on tap there, as the wreath proclaims; bad wine no doubt, for good wine needs no bush. The little hatchet hangs out there, the one for which, in the proverb, the lazy carpenter is searching; and the bell hangs there too whose tolling, called *luien* in Dutch, is punningly identified with *luien* meaning "lazy people." This, therefore, is the haunt of Sloth, which seeks escape from boredom in drinking and fornication. The two-horned headdress of the woman under the curtain is in Brueghel's drawings the mark of the procuress. The owl, the bird of Minerva, goddess of wisdom, is fouling this nest of iniquity. Down below mouse-like merrymakers are dancing to a fiddler's music. The top of the barrel above them wears a man's face, the bunghole its nose, two holes the eyes, an effect that is enhanced by the hat that hangs over it. Gluttony is portrayed by the man who is turning the spit from behind the screen that protects him from the heat; that is

abundantly clear from his being accompanied by a hog with a winged demon astride on his back. The voracious fish and the toad are also emblems of insatiable greed.

The most conspicuous figure in the landscape is the giant man-egg that crawls along the water's edge. A colossal figure sits astride upon its back, his legs and the upper part of his body protruding through the holes in the shell. The man-egg's posterior is a gaping hole which a crowd of people—Lilliputians in respect to this oval Gulliver—invade with a ladder and a huge knife. The spurred rider, who carries a sword at his hip, wears a cardinal's hat marked on its brim with the keys of St. Peter. But this cardinal's body is as empty a shell as the one that serves him as a mount. It has a wide crack in the back through which a tree grows out of him; has grown would be more correct, for its branches are apparently all dead. A flying dragon with a fish's head comes charging at him from the sky. But the cardinal maintains a Job-like patience. The church on his left is on fire, all kinds of sprites and devils and demons are haunting human life on land and water, and in the hollow tree of life man is the victim of his own evil passions. But the imperturbable cardinal turns his back on all that pageantry of evil and looks towards the horizon where the city's churches, in the light of the rising sun, point their crosses heavenward, calling for trust in God by which men are able to endure the vicissitudes of mortal life. For Patience, says the Latin legend, "is to endure with equanimity the evils which are inflicted or befall."

PATIENCE.

PATIENTIA.

H. Cock excude · 1557

Brueghel. Inuent.

PATIENTIA EST MALORVM QVÆ AVT INFERVNTVR AVT ACCIDVNT, CVM ÆQVANIMITATE PERLATIO Lact. Inst. Lib. 5

THE LATIN inscription says: "Faith most of all must be preserved, especially in regard to religion, for God is prior to and mightier than man." Faith occupies the centre of the scene carrying the tables of the Law on her head and the New Testament in her right hand. She stands on top of the open tomb, her feet on the stone that was taken away from the sepulchre. Around her are the instruments of Christ's passion: the whipping post and the scourge, the coat without seam and the dice with which the soldiers cast lots for it, the hammer that nailed Jesus to the cross. By the whipping post stands the water can and the basin in which Pilate washed his hands; on it stands the cock that crowed when Peter had denied his Master; on the edge of the tomb the flasks of ointment of the three Maries; and in the right foreground lies the bag with the thirty pieces of silver for which Judas Iscariot betrayed Him.

The nimbused bird on the right shoulder of Faith is the Phœnix, symbol of the resurrection. Behind her are the spear that pierced the Lord's side, the lance with the sponge soaked in vinegar, and the ladder that was used in the descent from the Cross. In the left aisle the sacraments are administered, in the central nave a devout congregation of the faithful is listening to the preaching of the gospel.

FIDES

Cock exc.   Brugel Inu.

FIDES MAXIMÈ À NOBIS CONSERVANDA EST RRAECIPVE IN RELIGIONEM,
QVIA DEVS PRIOR ET POTENTIOR EST QVAM HOMO.

HOPE IS SEEN in the centre foreground standing on an anchor, her traditional symbol, and carrying a beehive on her head, a spade in her right hand, and a sickle in her left. Hope is the mainstay of the tillers of soil and sea. The turbulent waves are lashing both the ships and the harbor. Man's life on land and ocean is beset by calamities, which he could not endure without the aid of hope. As the Latin text expresses it: "Most sweet is the persuasion of hope and most necessary to life in the midst of so many almost unendurable trials." Imprisonment and conflagration are the two calamities that Brueghel has chosen to depict in the scene on land. The prisoners, sustained by hope, are praying for release, the fire fighters bestir themselves at the risk of their lives in hope of saving the house. The pregnant woman and the expectant angler fit into this picture of hope's sustaining power. So does the crescent moon which rises above this scene of undespairing misery as a bright promise of fulfilment. And most significant symbol of all is the blinded falcon on the bars of the prison window, who stands hopefully waiting for the lifting of his hood. Thus the Christian upborne by hope in the darkness of this earthly prison awaits the moment when his eyes shall be uncovered and behold the eternal light of God.

HOPE.

SPES

IVCVNDISSIMA   EST   SPEI   PERSVASIO,   ET   VITAE   IMPRIMIS
NECESSARIA   INTER   TOT   AERVMNAS   PENEQ   INTOLERABILES.

CHARITY.

CHARITY STANDS in the centre of this scene, but no one in the crowd around is aware of her presence. For charity does good unobtrusively. Only two little children have recognized her. Children know by intuition goodness of heart. She reaches out to them with her right hand; in her left she holds a flaming heart. On her head stands the pelican who feeds her starving young with her heart's blood. The works of charity—a favorite subject of the early Dutch painters—are depicted in the surrounding scenes: the hungry are being fed, the thirsty laved, the naked clothed, the sick and bedridden cared for, the wandering pilgrims offered shelter, the prisoners comforted

CHARITAS

H. cock excude.

BRVEGEL 1559

SPERES TIBI ACCIDERE QVOD ALTERI ACCIDIT, ITA DEMVM EXCITABERIS AD OPEM FERENDAM
SI SVMPSERIS EIVS ANIMVM QVI OPEM TVNC IN MALIS CONSTITVTVS IMPLORAT

JUSTICE is represented by a young woman who carries a sword in her left hand and a pair of scales in her right. She is blindfolded because she passes judgment without respect of person. Her sightless face is turned towards the left foreground, where a suspect is being tortured on the rack. No age ever knew itself inhuman or cruel in administering justice. The judges of Brueghel's time were conscious of being severe but believed themselves to be righteous dispensers of justice. They did not condemn a man to death who was not a self-confessed evildoer. Hence a suspect who stood by his denial of guilt was put to the torture. They would acquit him if in the pain he still persisted in maintaining his innocence. To the right two youths are on trial before the *schepenbank,* the bench of echevins, the municipal judges. They have found them guilty of the charge, and the chief magistrate, behind the table, is reading the verdict, which is being recorded in the rolls by the *griffier,* the court secretary. The two convicts are listening to their death sentence, as they have been given a crucifix to hold while hearing judgment passed. Farther back on the platform, which is a kind of balcony in front of a city hall or court house, a poor wretch bends his head to kiss the crucifix as he awaits the blow of the executioner's sword, while a priest is praying for his soul; and in a recess to th[e] right a thief is having his hand chopped off as another [is] being led to the block for like punishment. On a scaffold i[n] the square below a man, tied to a stake, is being beaten wit[h] rods, and another is hoisted up, head downward, by h[is] hands and feet, which are tied together behind his back. I[n] the far background breakers of the law are atoning for the[ir] crimes on the wheel, the gallows, at the stake. The cross [of] Christ, raised on a pedestal on top of a hill, rises high abov[e] this scene of woe as a guarantee that justice thus admini[s]tered has the sanction of the Supreme Judge. For its aim [is] not revenge but the improvement and protection of societ[y.] The Latin text defines it thus: "It is the aim of the law tha[t] it shall correct him whom it punishes, or that his punish[-] ment shall make the others better, or that, after the elimina[-] tion of the wicked, the rest shall live the more securely.["] Brueghel has expressed in the faces of magistrates, law off[i-] cers, and spectators that they are not prompted by cruelt[y] or lust for vengeance. No one takes pleasure in the scene[.] They all look serious and aware of the solemnity of the pro[-] ceedings. One realizes that the essence of the grim spectac[le] is not the death of a criminal but the law triumphant in hi[s] punishment.

JUSTICE.

SCOPVS LEGIS EST, AVT VT EV QVE PVNIT EMENDET, AVT POENA
EIVS CAETEROS MELIORES REDDET AVT SVBLATIS MALIS CAETERI SECVRIORES VIVAT.

PRUDENCE.

I F YOU WANT to be prudent, you must keep your mind on the future and consider all possible contingencies." That is the meaning of the Latin legend. The sieve, the convex mirror, and the coffin, which are the attributes of Prudence, show her mindful of possible waste, of oncoming age, and of death. She stands on a couple of ladders which lie flat on the ground. These and the buckets by her feet were the indispensable precautions against the danger of fire, which in Brueghel's time, when most houses were built of wood, was much greater than now. The woman in the left foreground is keeping the fire under the pot within bounds with a dash of water. To the right, farm people are busily stocking the larder and cellar wit winter provisions, the attic with fuel; and the farmer i the background is repairing his house to keep out the wir ter cold. In the distance others are repairing the sea dik To the left a dying man is making his testament; the do tor who is examining his water has evidently given hir small hope. The money chest and the watchdog are saf guards that the prudent will not do without. In the righ hand corner the artist has drawn a porridge bowl in whic a spoon stands straight up like a mast upon the deck. Tha is an allusion to a popular Dutch ditty expressive of one joy in knowing his tomorrow secure.

PRVDENTIA

SI PRVDENS ESSE CVPIS, IN FVTVRVM PROSPECTVM OSTENDE, ET
QVAE POSSVNT ESSE CONTINGERE, ANIMO TVO CVNCTA PROPONE

THE CHIEF attribute of Fortitude is the anvil, unflinching target of hammer blows. The artist, thus, has placed it on her head. By virtue of her very nature she can bear the heavy load. Another attribute is the pillar, a third the chain by which the Dragon of Evil is held in check. She stands on the monster's neck and for greater security its tail is caught between the planks of a press.

Fortitude alone among the seven virtues has been endowed by the artist with angel's wings. She must rise above the passions and overcome the vices they engender. For, as the Latin has it, "To control one's own temper, to restrain anger, and contain the other vices and passions is true fortitude." Hence the battlefield in the midst of which the maiden stands unmoved by her pillar presents the onslaught of her faithful upon the seven cardinal vices. The proud peacock, the gluttonous swine, the slothful ass, the lascivious monkey, the angry bear, the envious dog, the avaricious toad are being gorged by Fortitude's warriors. The fortress in the centre background, with its four towers that look like human faces, is the citadel of Man. The mouth and the eyes are the gate and the windows through which temptation may enter. But Fortitude has manned the walls; her angels guard the bastions. In front of the moat the hellish host of vices and passions, which has assailed the fortress with battle rams and other medieval weapons of attack, are being routed by the storm troops of Fortitude. They are driven back into their shell.

FORTITVDO

ANIMVM VINCERE, IRACVNDIAM COHIBERE CAETERAQ VITIA ETAFFECTVS
COHIBERE VERA FORTITVDO EST·

TEMPERANCE STANDS in the middle foreground, a clock on her head, a bit in her mouth, the reins in her right hand, and a pair of spectacles in her left. The clock affords a check on the passage of time, the bit and the reins are a check on the impatient horse, the spectacles a check on our faulty vision. She stands on the wing of a windmill, which catches the wild wind and tempers its force to man's use. All around her the seven liberal arts, grammar, logic, rhetoric, arithmetic, music, astronomy, and geometry, are represented in activities as practiced by their adepts.

Brueghel's own art is not forgotten: behind the students of arithmetic in the left foreground a young painter armed with palette and mahlstick, is seated in front of his easel. On the primitive stage in the left background the fool tempers the austerity of the morality play with his wit. "Let us show," says the Latin text, "that we are not given to vain pleasure, nor spendthrifts, nor lustful, and that we do not live, with a miser's tenacity, in sordidness and ignorance." Application to the study of the various disciplines of the schools tempers the passions and makes for a well-balanced and temperate life.

TEMPERANCE.

VIDENDVM, VT NEC VOLVPTATI DEDITI PRODIGI ET LVXVRIOSI
APPAREAMVS, NEC AVARA TENACITATI SORDIDI AVT OBSCVRI EXISTAMVS

THE
BIG
FISHES
EAT
THE
LITTLE
ONES.

Page 40.

EVER SINCE the early Middle Ages the Dutch have been fishermen and drawn wealth from the sea. Hence the fish and the net that traps them occur frequently in Dutch figures of speech. The boy in the boat with the knife between his teeth has just discovered that there is truth in the proverb that his father has taught him: "See, son," the old man says, "I have known for a long time that the big fish eat the little ones," and he points, as he says it, to the stranded giant which like a horn of plenty disgorges an avalanche of all sorts of sea food, all of which have been preying on still smaller creatures of their own kind. The angler on the beach is using a little fish as bait for a big one, and a large glutton in the foreground is swallowing a smaller one which is swallowing another of still smaller size. Marine life is graded mass murder, the old fisherman knows too well, and a counterpart of man's inhumanity to man. Idinau, the compiler of a book of Dutch proverbs that was published by Plantijn at Antwerp in 1606, explains the proverb as a reflection on the rich who suppress the poor. But he adds, for the latter's solace, that one day the gluttons will receive their reward. Brueghel's picture implies the same comfort. The knife with which the helmeted storm trooper charges into the giant's belly is marked with the token that signifies the world. The world will at last confound the oppressor and force him to surrender his spoils as the sea tyrant in Brueghel's picture must do. The underfish of our day are still at the mercy of the big gluttons, but they are preyed upon with a subtler and seemingly benevolent voracity. Big nations gobble up little ones to save them from this or that poisonous Ism; big corporations, holding companies, chains, department stores swallow up the little fellows for the general public's and the little fellows' own good. Besides, we moderns are blessed with a knowledge that was not within the reach of Brueghel's contemporaries. A century after him the microscope revealed to Anthonie van Leeuwenhoek that the pupa of a flea is sometimes attacked and fed upon by a tinier mite, a discovery that suggested to Jonathan Swift the often quoted lines:

> Nat'ralists observe a flea
> Hath smaller fleas that on him prey,
> And these have smaller still to bite 'em,
> And so proceed ad infinitum.

The system of graded voracity that was obvious to Brueghel's age has its counterpart in reverse in the microbic world. That invisible warfare, no less cruel and relentless than that of the fishes, presents another allegory of the human scene. Though the big ones eat the little ones, the little ones have the numbers and the power of persistence to prey upon their oppressors. Each evil, it would seem, creates in the reaction it calls forth a remedy for itself, but the remedy, alas, is all too often a new evil.

·GRANDIBVS EXIGVI SVNT PISCES PISCIBVS ESCA·

Siet sone dit hebbe ick zeer langhe gheweten dat die groote vissen de cleyne

Y OU MAY send an ass to school, but if he is an ass he will not come back a horse": the Dutchman's picturesque way of saying, "Once a fool, always a fool." Brueghel's picture repeats the illustration of its lesson in a number of details. Try to teach an ass to sing, he will only bray when the lesson is over. Give him a lighted candle, he will not see any the better. Give him a pair of spectacles, he will not know how to use them. The ass's human fellow scholars are his peers in asininity. One has studied the alphabet, but he is not wise enough to know that he must not stick his head into a beehive. Another gets the basket on his head, a symbolic act of dismissal. A couple are foolish enough to let themselves be caught under a hat.

"Two fools under one hood," says the proverb of those who are paired in folly, and another describes a meek fool as "easily caught under a hat." These two are defenseless simpletons who deserve to be crowned with a peacock' feather, for that was among humanists the badge of pusillanimity and cowardice, since they wrongly connected the Latin word *pavo,* meaning peacock, with the Latin verb *paveo* which means, "I am afraid." All the schoolmaster' pupils have passed through at least four of the stages of man, but school and life have not taught them anything. They are morons who will remain fools to the end. Among them the wise are out of place. In the school of asses and idiots the intellect is put behind bars.

Bruegel · Inuentor ·

COCK · EX · 1557

PARISIOS STOLIDVM SI QVIS TRANSMITTAT ASELLVM · SI HIC EST ASINVS NON ERIT ILLIC EQVVS

Al reÿst den esele ter scholen om leeren ist eenen esele hÿ en sal gheen peert weder keeren

BATTLE OF MONEY-POTS AND STRONG-BOXES.

Go to ye money boxes, barrels and chests! It is all for gold and good, this fighting and quarreling! Though they tell you differently, don't you believe it. That's why we carry the lance which never failed us. They are looking for means to put us down; but there would be no wars if there were nothing to plunder." All wars are engendered by greed. It is not the poor who make war, but the rich who want to rob each other. The possession of wealth engenders greed for more, and supplies to the greedy the means to satisfy their craving. Strong-boxes and barrels filled to the brim with gold ducats make the best armies. Those are the forces that clash on each battle-field.

Their owners would have us believe that they go to war for noble causes, for freedom, or justice, or the Church of Christ. But do not believe them. They go to war to steal more of the wealth that enables them to make war. It is a chain that has no end. For victory will give them new riches that will be coveted by others, their defeat will make them covet the lost spoils. Thus each war engenders another war. The clash between the money-pots and the strong-boxes knows no truce.

P. Bruegel Inuet.

Quid modo diuitiæ, quid fului vasta metalli
Congeries, nummis arca referta nouis,
Wel aen Ghy, Spaerpotten, Tonnen, en Kisten
Tis al om gelt en goet, dit striden en twisten.

Illecebres inter tantas, atq agmina furum,
Inditium cunctis efferus vncus erit,
Al seetmen v ooc anders, willet niet ghelouen,
Daerom vuere wy den haec die ons noyt en miste,

Præda facit furem, seruens mala cuncta ministrat
Impetus, et spolijs apta rapina feris.
Men soeckt wel actie om ons te verdoouen,
Maer men souwer niet krygen, waerder niet te roouen.

A LL YE WHO are lazy and gluttonous, be ye peasant, soldier or scholar, get to the land of Cockaigne and taste there all sorts of things without any labor. The fences are sausages, the houses covered with cakes; capons and chickens fly around ready-roasted." Thus says the rhyme underneath the print. The Dutch call this dreamland of loafers *Luilekkerland,* i.e., Lazy-and-lickerish-Land, and they say that it cannot be reached unless you eat your way towards it through the *Rijstenbrijberg,* the Rice-Pudding Mountain. In the background on the left a lazy glutton is tumbling out of the tunnel he has dug with his mouth. A roasted chicken has dropped on a plate set ready on a napkin on the sausage-fenced lawn, and in the right hand background another flies into the mouth of a farmer's wife who takes her ease by resting her arms on a soft cushion. Notice the cakes that tile the sloping roof over her head. The sleeping trio on the lawn present a loathsome picture of surfeit. They have thrown away their tools, the scholar his book, the peasant his flail, the soldier his lance, and are past all enjoyment. The empty eggshell hopping in the foreground is a symbol of their lives: empty eggshells all of them.

P. Breugel.
inuentor.

Die dâr luÿ en lacker sÿt bôr crijsman oft clercken
die gheraeckt daer en smaeckt clâr van als sonder werken

Die tuÿnen sÿn worsten die huÿsen met vlaÿen
cappuÿnen en kieckens tvliechter al ghebraÿen

THE FRENCH RHYME accompanying this engraving says, "When the merchant wants to take his rest, the monkeys offer his wares for sale." Hose, bags, gloves, mirrors, spectacles, shoelaces, buttons, rosaries, knives in sheaths, drums, horns, dice, hobby-horses, all have come out of one of his hampers, and two ransackers have crept inside the empty carrier and have great fun in rocking themselves back and forth. The other hamper is still being unpacked, and one of the looters sits among its wares examining a pair of spectacles. Another is trying on a pair of hose; a third is looking at his reflection in a mirror; a fourth is fouling the merchant's plumed hat; while a fifth as if to make amends for that outrage, is picking the sleeper's unkempt shock of hair clean of unwelcome visitors. Two playful ones are riding hobby-horses; and in the background a quartet is executing a country dance to the accompaniment of drum and horn music. More business-like companions of the dancers are exhibiting the merchant's stock on the branches.

And while his wares are thus being monkeyed with the merchant is blissfully asleep and probably dreaming of the profits from his sales.

QVAND. LE MERCIER SON DOVLX REPOS VEVLT PRENDRE, EN VENTE LES SINGES SES MARCHANDISES VONT TENDRE

A PICTURE of human selfishness. "Everyone seeks himself everywhere in everything. How then can anyone remain lost? In the tug of war each tries to get the long end of the rope, one pulling from above, the other from below. No one knows himself in this world. A strange spectacle for those who have their eyes open." These bits of wisdom are expressed in Latin, French, and Dutch in the verses that go with the print, and are illustrated in various ways in the picture. The bearded man in the barrel is not Diogenes, though he wanders around with a lantern. His name is *Elck,* that is Everyman, and he is not looking for a man, but for himself and his own advantage. He seeks it in his games, in chess and backgammon, in card games and dicing. He looks for it in his trade and business. Everyman is out for his own profit. His sacks, and hampers, and barrels, and packing cases are filled and traded and shipped for profit. He weighs and measures the wares he buys and sells so as to determine the profit he can get out of them. It is a tug of war between *Elck* and *Elck,* between buyer and seller, and their tug of war often turns into actual war between armed camps of soldiers. But no one in this self-seeking world knows himself. Thus says the legend under the framed picture on the wall which shows a man, in the midst of a jumble of his possessions, looking in a mirror and wondering whose face he sees. He will never know until the candle of his life is burnt down to the socket.

EVERYMAN.

NIEMAT·EN·KENT·HE·SELV

NEMO NON

H·COCK·EXCVD·CVM·PRIVILEG

Nemo non quærit passim sua commoda, Nemo   Nemo non inhiat priuatis vndique lucris,
Non quærit sese cunctis in rebus agendis,   Hic trahit, ille trahit, cunctis amor vnus habendi est

Sur le monde vn chacun par tout recherche,   Vn chacun pour le plus long tire aussy,   Elck soeckt hem seluen in alderley saken   Elck treckt oock om dlanckste soomen hier siet
Et en toutes choses Soymesme veut trouuer.   L'vn par haut & l'autre par bas s'efforce.   Ouer al de werelt, al wort hy gheuloeckt   Geen van bouen, dander van ondere.
Veu qu'vn chacun donques tousiours se cherche, Nul se cognoist Soymesme presque en ce monde icy: Hoe can dan iemant verdoelt gheraken   Niemant en kent schier hem seluen niet
Pourroit quelqu'vn bien perdu demeurer?   Ce bien noté sesmerueiller est force.   Als elck hem seluen nu altijt soeckt.   Siet wel aenmerckt die siet groot wondere.

ERASMUS WAS not too fond of his native country and often spoke contemptuously of its climate and its people. But once, in his "Adagia," he went out of his way to praise his fellow Dutchmen. "The Netherlanders are anything but rustic; on the contrary, to judge from their domestic life, they, more than other nations, are inclined to benevolence and courtesy and show less capacity for cruelty and fury. They are outspoken, they neither cringe nor simulate, and have no cardinal vices, except, perhaps, an addiction to the pleasures of the table. But no wonder that they succumb to their appetites. For they live in the midst of an incredible abundance of things that stimulate the desire for self-indulgence."

The household that keeps a meagre kitchen is consequently an object of popular scorn. *Schraalhans is daar keukenmeester,* the neighbors will say, "Lean-Hank is chef there." The lean kitchen of Brueghel's picture is no place for the fat bon-vivant who has entered there by mistake. The couplets in French and Dutch shown in the engraving are spoken by him. "Where Lean-fellow stirs the pot," he says, "there is poor feasting. I am running to the fat kitchen with a happy heart."

On. Maygre-os le pot moue, n̄t vu poure Conuiue
Pomre, à Grasse-cuisine iray, tant que ie Viue

Daer magherman die pot roert is een arm ghasterye
dus Loop ick nae de vette Cuecken met herten blue

THE FAT KITCHEN.

THE FAT KITCHEN is in every detail the counterpart of the previous scene. Lean-fellow stirs a tiny pot which seems almost empty; here three are hanging over the fire and a pig is being roasted on the spit. The gluttons around the table are bursting out of their skins; and the cat and dogs vie with their masters in corpulence. The bagpipe hung deflated on the wall in Lean-Hank's kitchen, as an emblem of under-nourishment. He carries it over his shoulder when he enters among the bonvivants. But they do not want his company: "Go away, Lean-fellow, hence, hungry though you are. It is here Fatkitchen, you don't belong here." Each of them is a blown-up bagpipe played upon by their appetites, each a human sausage stuffed to the splitting point. The garland of sausages round the neck of the fat fellow in the center is a miniature replica of the ring around the table.

piter brueghel inue

H. Cock excudeb

1563

Hors dici Maigre–dos á eunr hideuse mine
Tu nas que faire ici Car cest Graſſe-Cuisine

Vuech magherman uan hier hoe hongherich ghij siet
Tis hier al uette Cuecken ghij en dur hier niet.

YE PEOPLE of Malleghem, be well disposed. I, Dame Witch, want to be loved here too. I have come here to cure you, at your service, with my proud assistant. Let the great and the small come without tarrying, if ye have the wasp in the head or are plagued with the stone."

Thus speaks the witch in the doggerel that accompanies the picture. Malleghem is a township in Flemish Belgium. Since *Mal* is a Dutch word for foolish or mad, popular wit has declared Malleghem to be the home of fools. Those nitwits who believe the quack doctor's boast that he has salves and remedies for all ills are said to be citizens of Malleghem. The witch of Malleghem offers to relieve their brains of the stone or the buzzing wasp. Such gullibility is grist to the deceiver's mill in the background. The witch is seen performing an operation on a country clown's jaw, and a crowd of sore-mouthed louts are waiting for their turn to be duped.

Another fool has been tied to a chair and will be relieved of the stone on his brain. The same operation is being performed on an idiot in the broken egg shell in the right foreground. In the opposite corner two wise men shake their hooded heads over such folly. *Mundus vult decipi,* the world asks to be deceived. A sceptic owl on top of the stone wall sits pondering. All people, it seems, are prisoners of their superstitions.

N·COCK·EXCVD·CVM·PRIVILEGIO·1559

Ghy lieden van Mallegem wilt nu wel syn ghesint   Om v te genesen ben ick gecomen hier.   Compt vry den meesten met den minsten sonder verbeyen
Ick Vrou Hexe wil hier oock wel worden bemint   Tuwen dienst. met myn onder meesterssen fier   Hebdy de wesp int hooft, oft loteren v de keyen.

THE ALCHEMIST.

THIS PICTURE, one of Brueghel's finest compositions, tells the same story told by the Canon's
Yeoman in Chaucer's "Canterbury Tales." There
is the alchemist mixing ingredients at his work bench, his
apprentice blowing the fire, his poor wife shaking the last
coins out of her purse to buy materials for the final experi-
ment, which is bound to succeed; and at his desk the scholar
whose book learning guides their will-o'-the-wisp quest for
gold. In the background, through the open window, the
artist shows us where the quest will end: in the poorhouse.

DEBENT IGNARI RES FERRE ET POST OPERARI
IVS LAPIDIS CARI VILIS SED DENIQЗ RARI
VNICA RES CERTA VILIS SED VBIQЗ REPERTA

QVATVOR INSERTA NATVRIS IN NVBE REFERTA
NVLLA MINERALIS RES EST VBI PRINCIPALIS
SED TALIS QVALIS REPERITVR VBIQЗ LOCALIS

TIME, ON AN hour glass, drives his chariot, pulled by the horses of the Sun and Moon, across the spoils of the world. In his left hand he raises a serpent biting its tail, the ancient symbol of the circular course of mortal life that revives after death by new birth. The child that he carries on his right shoulder betokens that principle of constant renewal. He passes by the twelve signs of the Zodiac: Sagittarius, Capricornus, Gemini, Virgo, Libra, Scorpio, Aquarius, Leo, Pisces, Taurus, Aries, and Cancer. These are depicted on the globe, whose axis is the tree of life. A clock, suspended from one of its to branches, ticks off the minutes of Time's passage. Th horses' hoofs and the wheels of the chariot crush the ha diwork of man that litters the road. Time snatches ever thing, or leaves what he does not snatch to Death, wh armed with his sickle, follows Time on an emaciate mount.

In the track of Time and Death follows Fame riding o an elephant and blowing her clarion to the four wind All that remains of man's deeds is a breath of wind.

TEMPVS OMNIA ET SINGVLA CONSVMENS.

Petrus Bruegel inuen.

Io Galle
excudebat

Solis equus, Lunæque, inuectum quattuor Horis,
Signa per extenti duodena volubilis Anni,

Proripiunt Tempus: curru quod præpete secum
Cuncta rapit: comiti Morti non rapta relinquens.

Pone subit, cunctis rebus Fama vna superstes,
Gætulo boue vecta, implens clangoribus orbem.

Mopsus is an Arcadian shepherd who figures in Virgil's eighth Eclogue. His rival Damon bemoans in song the loss of his sweetheart Nisa, and the Latin words that go with the picture are taken from his ironic complaint: "Mopsus is marrying Nisa. What may we not hope for, we lovers!" Brueghel did not intend to give an illustration of that pastoral wedding. He scorned the idyllic fancies of Arcady and opposed to them a realistic scene from the life of the poor in rural Flanders. The analogy between his Mopsus and Virgil's is merely accidental. The Dutch word *mops,* meaning a small, flat-nosed breed of bulldog, was also applied to a country lout; its latinized form *mopsus* made the Flemish bumpkin the namesake of Virgil's Arcadian shepherd, but the two have nothing else in common. The boor has no poetry in him, though even such as he are capable of falling in love. *Men vond nooit leelijk lief* (there never was an ugly sweetheart) says the Dutch proverb, for love is blind, and Idinau, who quotes it in his collection, adds "no wonder then that every simple Simon finds a slut" (*dat hannen oock een sloor vindt*). What may we not hope for then, we lovers?

The wedding feast is evidently over, to judge by the bones and the egg and mussel shells that litter the foreground, and now the bride is being danced to bed as was the custom in those days. They will lie on the bare ground under the ragged makeshift tent. That rustic bower flies a little vane in honor of the wedding feast. The castle in the background with its smoking chimney supplies a mocking contrast to this scene of wretchedness and destitution. Did Brueghel intend to suggest by the shutter off its hinges that the world which presented such stark contrasts was sadly out of joint?

MOPSO NISA DATVR, QVID NON SPEREMVS AMANTES.

Y E NUMBSKULLS who are plagued with vanity, come to the fore if you like to go bowling. Although one love honor and another his money, the world praises the greatest numbskulls. Numbskulls are found in every nation, though they do not wear a foolscap on their pate, who take such pleasure in dancing that their foolish head turns like a top. The foulest numbskulls waste all their substance. There are some who take others by the nose. One sells trumpets, another spectacles, with which they deceive many nitwits. Yet there are numbskulls who behave wisely and grasp the true sense of numbskulling; because they enjoy their own foolishness their numbskull will hit the goal pin best." So say the verses.

At the feast of fools the bowling alley is the chief attraction. That does not mean that Brueghel despised bowling as a foolish sport. The connection between bowling and folly is brought about by a pun. The word *bol* means both "ball" and "head," and *sottebol* means "foolish head," "numbskull." They all come to the feast, each carrying his own ball, his *sottebol*. In the centre a male and a female fool "take one another by the nose," an idiomatic expression for "fooling one another." The scene is a pleasure garden such as in Brueghel's day could be found in the environs of the prosperous cities of wealthy Flanders.

P: Brueghel Inuentor.   cum gratia et Priuilo.

Ghÿ Sottebollen, die met ÿdelheÿt, ghequelt ſÿt.	Men vint' Sottebols, onder elcke nacie,	De vuÿſſte Sottebols, lappent al duer de billen,	Al ſÿnder Sottebols, die haer wÿſelÿck draghen,
Compt al ter banen, die luſt hebt om rollen,	Al en draghen ſy gheen ſotſcappen op haeren cop	Dan ſÿnder, die d'een dander, metten muſe votten.	En van tSottebollen, den rechten ſin ſmaken
Al wordet dien ſÿ tere en dander tghelt quÿt	Die int danſen hebben, al ſulken gracie	De ſulck, vercoopt trompen, en dander brillen	Om dat ſÿ in hun ſelfs ſotheÿt hebben behagen
De weerelt die vrÿſt, de grootſte Sottebollen	Dat hunnen Sottebol, drayet, ghelÿck eenen top	Daer ſÿ veel, Sottebollen, mede verſchatten	Sal hueren Sottebol alder beſt de pin raſen.

THE STORY of St. James and Hermogenes is told in "The Golden Legend" by Jacobus de Voragine. After the ascension of Our Lord, James preached the gospel in Judea. The Pharisees appealed for aid against him to the magician Hermogenes, who sent his disciple Philetus to confront the apostle and prove him an impostor before the Jews. But the very reverse happened: Philetus returned to his master a convert to the faith in Christ. The enraged magician ordered the demons to bring James before him and chain both him and Philetus. But when they came flying to James they howled: "Apostle James, have pity on us, for behold, we burn before our time." James asked the angel of God to release them and ordered the demons to bring Hermogenes bound before him. They obeyed and said to James: "Give us power over him, that we may avenge thine insults and our burnings." And James answered: "Here is Philetus, why do you not seize him?" And they replied: "We can not touch so much as an ant that is in thy chamber." Whereupon James turned to Philetus and said: "Let us follow the example of Christ, who taught that we should return good for evil. Hermogenes bound thee, do thou free him." Then James gave him his staff and he went off and brought his books on magic to the apostle to be burnt. But James commanded him to throw them into the sea. And when he had done this, he threw himself at the apostle's feet and said: "Receive as a penitent him whom thou hast succoured even when he envied and slandered thee." It was a story that evidently appealed to Brueghel because of the apostle's insistence that good should be returned for evil. He placed the saint in the centre of the scene, clothed in the garb worn by pilgrims to his shrine at Compostella: the long cape, the pilgrim's pouch dangling from the girdle, the water bottle attached to the wrist, and the long staff, the saint's traditional attribute, which according to the legend had been handed to him by Christ himself. The demons have seized hold of Hermogenes, but the apostle raises his hand and orders them to desist.

Bruegel · inuent

Cock excudebat · 1 55

DIVVS IACOBVS DIABOLICIS PRAESTIGIIS ANTE MAGVM SISTITVR

THE OVERTHROW OF THE MAGICIAN.

THERE IS NOTHING in the legend as told by Jacobus de Voragine to which this picture serves as an illustration. Brueghel did not intend it to depict an episode in the story; he evidently meant to convey the idea that the magic pageantry of this world, being nothing but a juggler's make-believe, is overthrown when confronted with God's truth. He shows us a mad kermis scene, such as every town in Flanders witnessed when it celebrated the anniversary of the dedication of one of its churches. A conjurer is performing tricks at a table, tight-rope walkers, contortionists, acrobats, trained monkeys, and exotic animals are among the attractions, and for those who like horrors the magician will cut off a man's head and put it back in place, no doubt, without any harm done. A fool beats a drum to call the gullible to this scene of folly. It is a show that caters to the evil appetites of man and unchains in him the demons by which he is possessed. The great deceiver, the prestidigitator who manipulates this show, has power over them and orders them to work his will. But when he is confronted by the man of God they are turned from his tools into his tormentors. The make believe kermis scene of Vanity Fair, this world of human folly, will be overthrown by its own vices, which are but agents of God's will.

Cock excudebat 1565

Bruegel inuent

IDEM IMPETRAVIT A DEO VT MAGVS A DEMONIBVS DISCERPERETVR

THE
DESCENT
OF
CHRIST
INTO
HELL.

JESUS SURROUNDED by angels descends into Hell in a blaze of light that frightens all the devils and demons. They flee in all directions and tumble over each other in their haste to escape. The doors of the mouth of hell are broken and the tormented souls are called out by the Saviour. The Latin text is from the twenty-fourth Psalm, the seventh verse:

"Lift up your heads, O ye gates; and be ye lift up, ye everlasting doors; and the King of glory shall come in."

TOLLITE ô PORTE, CAPITA VESTEA ATTOLLIMINI FORES SEMPITERNE ET INGREDIETVR REX ILLE GLORIOSV̄

IN GRYNAEUS' EDITION of Erasmus' *Adagia* a proverb is discussed that explains this strange picture: "When the head is sick the whole body suffers." The Greeks, says Grynaeus, expressed the idea this way: "The fish begins to rot at the head."

From the days of the early Christians Christ has been cryptically imaged as a fish. The rotten fish in Brueghel's picture represents the Church of Christ, and its head, of course, the papacy, the source of the corruption within the body of the Church. The process of decomposition has gone so far that drunkenness, manslaughter, and murder are rife among its members, and birds of rapine prey upon the corruption. But the tree that grows out of the fish's mouth is promise of new life, the Church of Christ being imperishable.

The ailing head is that of the body politic. By placing the fish on top of it, Brueghel implied that the power of the Church, even in its rotten state, transcends the secular power. The head is being washed ashore like a boat in distress; the two men in its mouth are trying to save it from sinking by baling out the water. The column of fire that flares up above their heads is the tongue of the human

wreck. The artist remembered the words from the Epistle of James, III, 6: "The tongue is a fire, a world of iniquity among our members, that it defileth the whole body and setteth on fire the course of nature." Hence all the ills that infect the body politic: revolt, wars, depraved morals. The head is being attacked by a gang of rebellious sailors, heralds are blowing alarm, or proclaim a declaration of war; in the distance an army is being disembarked from a floating turret of apparently oriental design; they are probably the Turks, then the dreaded menace of Europe. In the foreground nightmarish scenes that constitute this world of iniquity of which James speaks in his Epistle.

St. Anthony turns his back upon this vice-infected world. Inside the hollow tree King David is singing a psalm, the eleventh, and the saint, with raised hand, listens to its comforting prophecy: "In the Lord put I my trust: how say ye to my soul, Flee as a bird to your mountain? For lo, the wicked bend their bow, they make ready their arrow upon the string, that they may privily shoot at the upright in heart . . . The Lord trieth the righteous, but the wicked and him that loveth violence his soul hateth. Upon the wicked he shall rain snares, fire and brimstone . . ."

MVLTÆ TRIBVLATIONES IVSTORVM, DE OMNIBVS IIS LIBERABIT EOS DOMINVS· PSAL·33·

"Come, ye blessed of my Father, into the eternal Kingdom.

Go, ye cursed of my Father, into the everlasting fire."

CHRIST, SEATED on the rainbow, calls the chosen to heaven and sends the doomed into the mouth of hell, a vision of the Day of Judgment that was familiar to young and old. The mouth of hell was a common requisite of the stage set for a medieval passion play. Local artists were employed in designing the scenery, and the very best among them did not scorn to put their talent to work, Pieter Brueghel not excluded. I have no doubt that his help was often called in, for no one could create a gaping hell monster more suggestively. The happenings in the foreground remind one of the words in the Book of Revelation (XX, 13): "And the sea gave up the dead which were in it, and death and hell delivered up the dead which were in it." The owl that carries her nest on the back is doubtless the one of which Isaiah speaks in his description of the Lord's Day of Vengeance: "There shall the great owl make her nest and lay and hatch, and gather under her shadow." (XXXIV, 15).

VENITE. BENEDICTI. PATRIS. MEI. IN. REGNVM. ÆTERNVM.   Compt ghy ghebenedyde myns vaders hier
ITE. MALEDICTI. PATRIS. MEI. IN. IGNEM. SEMPITERNVM.   En ghaet ghy vermaledyde in dat eewighe vier.

Brueghel. inuet.   H. Cock. excude. cum priuileg. 1558.

TWELVE FLEMISH PROVERBS

I. *A leaking roof, a smoking fireplace, a cackling hen, and a quarrelsome woman are four household plagues.*

THE SERIES of twelve illustrations of proverbs of which this is the first was engraved by Ja[n] Wierix. None of them bears the name of Piete[r] Brueghel, whose drawings were the engraver's models. Th[e] proverbs are not quoted in their current form, but have i[n] each case been elaborated into rhyming doggerel that i[s] printed around the medal-shaped picture. At the foot o[f] some engravings a brief couplet in French sums up the gis[t] of the Dutch verse and thus achieves a near-translation o[f] the proverb that is illustrated. The first picture is self[-] explanatory. The legend around it says: "A leaking roo[f] and a smoking fireplace, by which the monkey sits an[d] watches, a crowing hen and a quarrelsome woman are mis[-] ery in the house and torment and grief."

Een leeckende dack ende een roockende schouwe, Ja daer de sinne welt sit en siet, En crayende hinne en tissende vrouwe Is ongheluck in huijs, ja quellinghe en verdriet

Femme qui tanse sans raison,
Ne fait quenuij a la maison

II. *All want to creep into the rich man's hole.*

TO CREEP into a man's hole" is a Dutch idiom meaning "to flatter." These crawlers are flatterers who hope to exchange their eulogies for the big man's money. For, says the circular rhyme: "He who has money to spend among the great and the small, and lets it run lavishly through his fingers, gets offices and all that he wants, for they all scramble to creep into his hole." Or as the French couplet expresses it more succinctly: "They wonder how they can get into the hole of him who has money to give away."

Die ghelt te gheuen heeft onder hooghe en slechte, En dat hij voet mit dat van sijnen schat, drusspen, Hij crijcht Officien in cout tsijnen rechte, Want dick en veel met hoe hem sal in tgat cruijpen.

On ne sait comme entrer on veut,
Au trou de cil qui donner peut.

III. *The world is full of deceit.*

THE FRENCH couplet makes the long-robed figure say, "I wear mourning because the world abounds in frauds." But he does not see that he is being robbed himself by the cutpurse world. The Dutch rhyme is more explicit: "Many a one mourns because the world is faithless. The greatest practise least justice and reason. Few live nowadays as they should. Robbery and trickery everywhere; everyone is a hypocrite." In the background a scene of highway robbery, and in the far distance the gallows, which is badly needed in such a faithless world. The windmill fits into this picture of robbery and trickery. The miller was a proverbial trickster. He was always suspected of returning to the farmer less than the full yield of his grain.

Je porte dueil voyant le monde,
Qui en tant de fraudes abonde.

Men rooft men treckt elck steeckt vol gheueijsde seden. ✚ De sulck draecht rou= om dat de Weerelt is onghetrou, Die meeste Bedrieghers mint recht en reden, Weynich leeftter nou, also hij leuen sou,

IV. *The rich man plays well upon a jawbone.*

THE IRONY of the proverb is clear: wealth can buy flattery. The French couplet says briefly: "He who hauls in the money plays well upon the jawbone," the Dutch lines, at greater length and less pointedly: "It is good to be on the receiving end in the general getting. The receiver fills the food bag and his work is praised. Though his wage be large, he knows how to get more; he lives in splendor and plays on the jawbone."

Tis goet Ontfangher sijn, inden Crijch principael: Hij vaf den Aessack en men laudere sijn sake, Al is sijn sagie groot noch weet hij sy dhael, Hij hout hem heerlijck en speelt op die kake

Qui de recevoir a moyen,
Sur la machoire ſ'ioue bien.

THE FAT MAN in the picture is not one of the gullible. "Look here," says the hawker according to the French couplet, "nets and trumpets and flutes, you never saw better ones." But the other answers: "Go away, go and sell your wares somewhere else." The Dutch text makes them say: "Look here, nets and trumpets and beautiful flutes; you can't find better ones in this country." "Go away, chapman, hawk somewhere else where the people are hearing deaf and seeing blind."

V. *Every tradesman praises his ware.*

A. Hier netten ende trompen ja oock schoon fluijten, Ghen bater waer men nu hier in d'landt en vindt. B. Weck versta e Cremer loopt elders stuijten, Daer t'volck noch is hoorende doof en siende blindt. ✚

A. Voicy des rets trôpes et flentes; Telle denree onques vous neutes.
B. Va ten mercier va ten dicy: Ven ailleurs ta denree aussi.

VI. *Knocking at a deaf man's door*.

THIS IS A proverbial idiom meaning "to plead in vain." The French rhyme says, "Now our begging is in vain for we cry at a deaf man's door." According to the Dutch text the mendicant at the closed door says, "No use knocking and praying, it is at a deaf man's door. Our stipend is getting scant, our hood is wearing out. Alas, the best has been eaten up. I will get rid of the sack."

Maintenant en vain nous mendions,
Car a lhuijs du sourd nous crions

VII. *Shooting one arrow after another.*

THE MEANING of this proverb is clearly explained by the French couplet: "He who often gives and gets no satisfaction from it shoots one arrow after another." The Dutch expands: "When one gives much and sees neither benefit nor improvement, it is no wonder that almost everyone gets annoyed. What is the use, since people have no self-control? One only shoots one arrow after the other." Charity that does not improve conditions is a senseless repetition of effort.

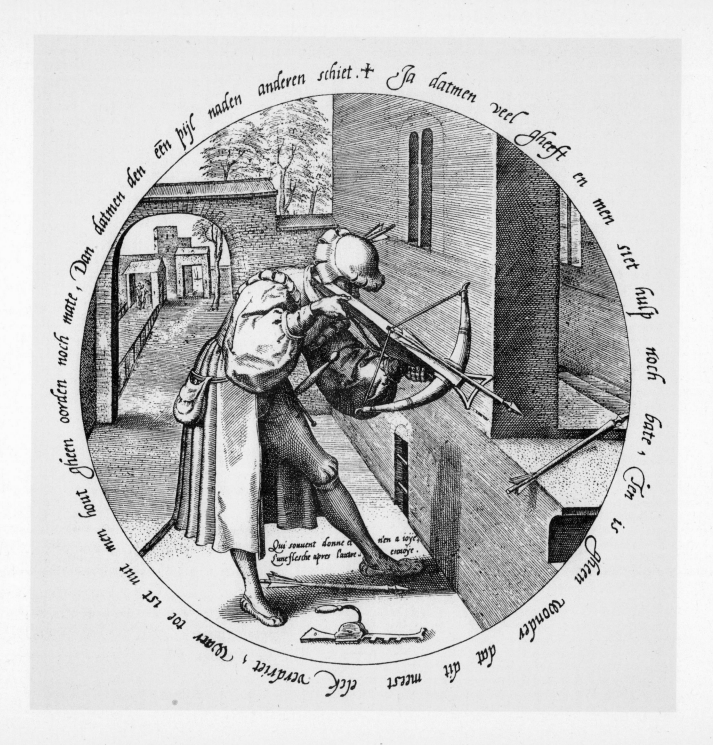

Ja datmen veel gheeft en men siet hulp noch bate, Ten is gheen wonder dat dit meest elck verdriet, Waer tot ist nut men hout gheen oorden noch mate, Dan datmen den een pijl naden anderen schiet. +

Qui souuent donne et n'en a ioye,
Lune flesche apres l'autre eiuoye.

VIII. *The blind leading the blind.*

T his is said of the incompetent who accept guid ance from the incompetent. The Dutch rhym implies that all mortals are blind and should trus only in God: "Walk always with great caution, be tru and trust no one but God in everything. For because on blind man leads the other, one sees them both together fal into the ditch."

IX. *A fool on top of a foul egg.*

THE DUTCH RHYME is addressed to foolish drunkards: "Fy, ye foolish drunkards all turned into bellies, always gulping it down and filling yourselves up to the throat; you sit like a fool on a foul egg and will end inside the empty shell."

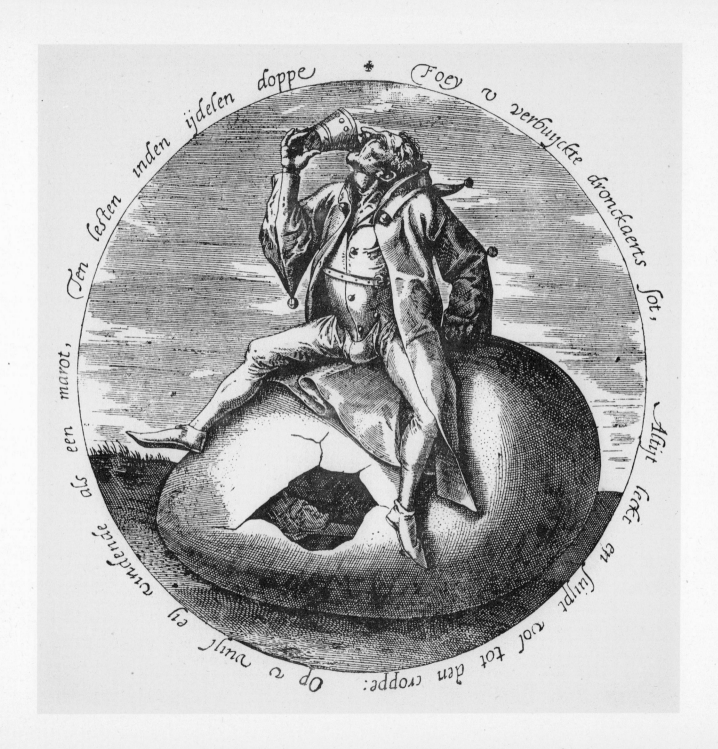

X. *He will sit by the bride scratching his head.*

THIS IS SAID of those who expect to get rich by cheating. The dishonest jeweler cheats himself, for the bride will despise his ware at the wedding. Says the Dutch rhyme: "He who fills his show case with fakes thinking to gain great wealth that way, verily, he will in the end lodge with Mr. Poor and, sitting by the bride, scratch his head."

Wie met bedroch sijn craem stoffeert, † Bij de bruijt sittende craut sijn noot

Bij de bruijt sittende craut sijn noot

Voorwaer hij ten leften met pouer logeert,

Voorwaer hij ten leften met pouer logeert,

En also meint te ghewinnen rijckdom groot:

XI. *The hay runs after the horse.*

THIS IS SAID of girls who run after the boys. The fellow in the background does not approve of such forwardness. He runs for safety to the house and will slam the door in the solicitor's face. The Dutch rhyme calls such conduct in a girl a disgrace: "It is wrong for the hay to run after the horse. Remember, ye daughters who go wooing without shame: It is not to your honor to court the boys. It is better when the horse runs after the hay."

XII. *He cares not whose house is on fire as long as he can warm himself by the coals.*

THIS IS SAID, of course, of those heartless people who seek to benefit by another's misfortune. "There are people," says the rhyme, "who selfishly and stupidly seek everyone's downfall without compassion. They care not whose house is on fire, as long as they can warm themselves by the coals."

The author gratefully acknowledges his indebtedness to René van Bastelaer's monumental publication *Les Étampes de Peter Bruegel l'Ancien,* to Max J. Friedländer's *Peter Bruegel,* to *Die Zeichnungen Pieter Bruegels* by Karl Tolnai, and to the article entitled *Brueghel's zeven deugden en zeven hoofdzonden (Beeldende Kunst* XXV, 1939) by J. G. van Gelder and Jan Borms.

A. J. B.

This book was designed by James Grunbaum.
Initials after Brueghel by Lili Cassell.
Engravings
The Metropolitan Museum of Art.
Set in Linotype Granjon by
The Composing Room, Inc.
Printed by H. Krauss, New York.
Bound by the Publishers Book Bindery.